The Clever Tykes® Books

Code-It Cody

Illustrated by Sam Moore

For anyone who loves to learn

Chapter 1: Error!

"Argh! No! Why isn't this computer working?" shrieked Miss Green.

She pushed lots of buttons on the keyboard.

She tapped the screen.

She even started waving her hands over her computer, as if trying to use magic. But nothing fixed the problem.

All Cody could hear was an irritating squeaking noise, rather like a giant magpie. He spun round to see Miss Green, squawking and flapping at her disobedient computer – again.

Cody's poor hearing often confused him. Sometimes he would mishear words and think something entirely different had been said. It certainly made life more interesting!

Cody stood up to help Miss Green but he made sure he took out his hearing aids first so he could concentrate properly! She was still flustered but gladly agreed. "This program won't load," she said, shaking her head. "You are our class expert for fixing computers, so please see what you can do."

After a quick click of the mouse and some tapping on the keyboard, Cody solved the problem in no time at all!

"There you go, Miss Green," he said modestly, popping his hearing aids back in. "Everything should be fine now."

Cody loved computers. Even when he was tiny, he wanted to learn more about how they worked. He became so good at using them that everyone asked for his help.

"Okay, class," said a relieved Miss Green. "Save your press releases and we will discuss them tomorrow."

The sounds of clicks and buzzes filled the room. Everyone had managed to save their work successfully. Well, almost everyone...

"Uh-oh," moaned Brad from the back of the classroom. "Miss Green! My computer screen has a strange message on it!"

Miss Green hurried to Brad's computer and began to shriek again - she didn't cope too well with computer errors. All the class had their hands over

their ears!

"Cody!" she whimpered. "Can you help?"

Cody studied Brad's computer screen, confident that he could solve the problem. But there, in huge, scary red letters, was the message:

ERROR CODE 2.357JKR

"Hmm, I've never seen that before," said a very puzzled Cody. This time, he had no idea what the problem was but he wasn't giving up just yet.

He pressed some buttons on the keyboard and the screen went black. He waited for a moment and pressed another key.

ERROR CODE 2.357JKR

"It didn't work!" said Miss Green, waving her arms around in panic. Everyone in the class fixed their eyes on Cody. Was he going to solve the problem?

"Aw, man. All my work is going to disappear, isn't it?" moaned Brad.

"Oh no!" cried Miss Green. "Cody, please save him!"

"Let me try something else," murmured Cody. He could feel everyone looking at him. The room had fallen silent but he wanted it to be noisy again. He wanted Miss Green to be a giant squeaky magpie again.

He pushed some other buttons on the keyboard. The screen turned green. Then yellow. Then purple. Another message popped up:

ERROR CODE 2.357JKR - FATAL ERROR

"A fatal error?!" Miss Green sounded like she was going to faint.

Cody gulped. The error was still there. What was he going to do?

2: The mysterious Mr Chip

"Cody, find the computer technician. Find Mr Chip!" shrieked Miss Green, who was still panicking.

Everyone began to whisper; they'd all heard of Mr Chip but no one had ever seen him.

Some believed that Mr Chip was actually a robot who zoomed around the school at night to fix broken computers. Others thought Mr Chip was a mechanical beast that ate old computers. Would the beast try to eat Cody's hearing aids, too?

Cody clutched his hands over his hearing aids and strolled out of the classroom.

"Cheers, mate," said Brad, giving Cody a reassuring pat on the back.

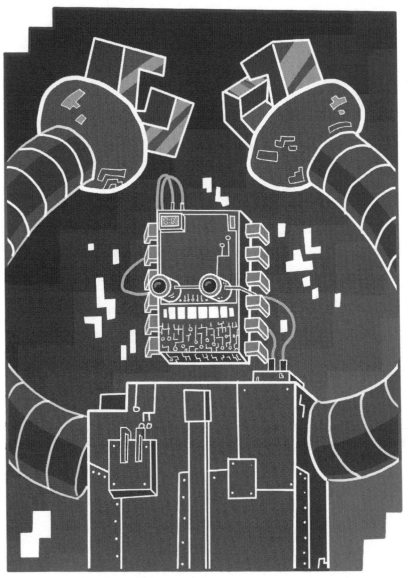

Mr Chip's office was hidden away in a distant corner

of the school. With each step, Cody edged further

away from the chatter and noise of the classrooms, and closer to the eerie unknown.

Lights flickered above him. Doors rattled and radiators hissed like snakes.

"If only I'd been able to fix that computer!" said Cody to himself. He breathed deeply and moved on, wondering who (or what) he might meet.

Eventually, Cody reached Mr Chip's office. Nobody else was around. He knocked the door just once. He heard nothing but the echo of the knock drifting down the corridor.

Then, there was a voice: a cold, menacing voice from inside the office.

"Come. In."

It didn't sound like a person at all.

"Don't be silly, Mr Chip can't be a robot!" Cody repeated to himself.

His hand shook as he slowly turned the door handle and carefully pushed open the door. He peered inside – no one was there.

He saw desks piled high with broken computers. Some monitors had wires sticking out of them, while others had screens filled with

random numbers and letters.

The room looked like a graveyard for computers!

"Hello? Mr Chip?" asked Cody nervously. He listened carefully but he heard nothing – not even the menacing voice from moments ago.

Then, he saw at the far side of the room a door that was ajar. Cautiously, Cody crept towards it when he suddenly heard that same cold voice: "Can. I. Help. You?"

Cody's eyes widened and his body froze. It was true! Mr Chip was a robot! He had to decide quickly what to do, before the robot ate his hearing aids.

His heart raced. He could hear shuffling – the robot was coming!

"Argh!" wailed Cody.

"Woah! Sorry. I didn't mean to scare you. I was just testing a new invention of mine," said a human voice.

Mr Chip appeared in the doorway. He looked very human and he had a beard and glasses. There were no wires or light bulbs screwed into his head – there was no robot in sight.

Mr Chip laughed as he placed the microphone he was using onto a nearby desk. "I wanted to experiment with my voice-changing machine - it still needs some work. How can I help?"

Cody sighed with relief before introducing himself. He felt silly for letting his imagination run wild.

"I'm Cody from Miss Green's class. There's an error on one of the computers."

"Cody, you say? I've heard all about you! Miss Green has told me you are quite the computer expert."

Cody reluctantly admitted that he didn't know how to solve the problem on Brad's computer.

"Not to worry!" said Mr Chip, as he screwed some loose panels back onto a laptop and patted it as though he'd just healed it. "I think it's fantastic that you tried to use your knowledge to help others.

"Have you ever thought about joining Computer Club? It's after school tomorrow. It will help you to develop your computer skills and it might even give

you some ideas of what to do when you grow up."

He handed Cody a leaflet with all the details about the club.

After gathering his tools and equipment, Mr Chip posed like a superhero and pointed to the door. "Let's go and fix that computer!"

"Erm, okay," said Cody. Mr Chip was definitely different from other grown-ups at school.

Chapter 3: Computer Club

Cody looked forward to his first visit to Computer Club all the next day. Sadly, it meant having to endure art, his least favourite lesson, before the end of school.

He grumpily used some charcoal to draw a cityscape. At least, it was supposed to be a cityscape.

Cody had forgotten to be careful and rubbed the charcoal too much, which left each building looking like a smudgy, dark blur.

Brad laughed. "Ha, mate. Is that supposed to be a forest at night?"

Cody glanced at the clock – it still wasn't time for Computer Club. All he wanted to do was escape from this anguish.

When the school bell eventually rang, Cody was so relieved that he charged across the school grounds to the I.T. rooms, excited that he was about to meet other people who liked computers as much as he did. He couldn't wait to discuss the latest gizmos and gadgets with them.

He opened the door to the Computer Club room and heard familiar buzzing and clicking. People were already there!

"Hi there, I'm Cody," he said, as he greeted the girl nearest to him. She

turned around in her chair and looked startled to
see the new boy.

"Who are you? You're not a member of this club, so
you need to tell Mr Chip you are here," she replied
abruptly. "Oh, I'm
Lucy."

She scrunched up her
face and turned back
to her computer.

"So, why did you join
Computer Club?"
Cody asked, hoping
Lucy would be a little
friendlier.

She shrugged her shoulders but looked up at him
thoughtfully.

"I told him that before," said Lucy. "He gets far too excited about the idea and doesn't think it through. I'm much more thoughtful."

Cody noticed another girl sitting at the far side of the room, hiding away from everyone else. She certainly wasn't jumping around the room or showing off.

"Who's that?" asked Cody.

"That's Hana. She doesn't say much but I hear she is one of the smartest kids in school," replied Lucy.

Cody was intrigued. He wandered over to Hana and introduced himself. She muttered something and looked down at her desk. He didn't hear what she said but he could tell that she was very shy.

Cody tried to make her feel comfortable: "I know what it feels like to be shy, Hana. When I first came to school, everyone gave me strange looks because I was wearing hearing aids.

"I used to stay in the library at lunchtime because I didn't like people staring at my ears so much."

Hana lifted her head up and looked at him.

"But I learned that my deafness is just part of who I am," he went on. "I hear you're one of the smartest kids in school. You shouldn't be shy about that!"

Hana giggled quietly. "Thanks, Cody," she whispered. Cody took a seat next to her, just as Mr Chip entered the room.

"Good afternoon, everyone," boomed Mr Chip cheerily. "I hope you all said hello to Cody. Would you believe, he used to think I was a mysterious robot?"

"Yeah, we all did!" chanted Owen. Everyone laughed, including Mr Chip.

"All right then. Let's get started!"

Chapter 4: What's coding?

"Is everyone ready?" asked Mr Chip. "Today I'm going to teach you all about coding!" He clapped his hands in excitement.

Cody checked his hearing aids. Both of them were switched on but he was confused. He quickly raised his hand. "Did you say you were going to teach everyone about *me*?"

Mr Chip smiled. "Oh, I'm sorry. I said 'coding', not 'Cody'. They do sound rather similar! I'll try to speak more clearly."

Hana smiled, too. Cody realised he must have sounded a bit silly but he didn't mind. He misheard things often and he found that it was always better to ask to be sure.

"If we want a computer to do interesting things, we need to make sure it knows what we're asking it to do," Mr Chip told the class. "Computer code is a language that computers can understand."

"But isn't coding really difficult, Mr Chip?" asked Lucy. "My big brother is learning about coding at university and he says it is really hard!" She sank her head into her hands in despair.

Owen dropped his head onto his desk. "Oh no, my brain is going to melt out of my ears. This is going to be hard, isn't it?"

"Don't worry, Lucy and Owen!" said Mr Chip. "We will start with the easy stuff first."

Owen lifted his head up off the table. "Will coding help me to build my footballer?" Owen still seemed set on creating his robot.

Mr Chip nodded. "Well, you will still need to find the metal and wires to build it but if you want your robot to know where to kick the football, you will need to use coding. In fact, can anyone suggest another interesting way that coding is used?"

Silence filled the room as everyone tried to think. Then, Hana, who had been very quiet, slowly raised her hand.

"Video games?" she asked softly.

Everyone looked up, surprised that Hana had spoken.

"Yes, of course," said Mr Chip cheerily. "Coding is used to program video games and apps. Games consoles are just like computers. They need coding so that they do the right things."

He went on to explain how many of the gizmos and gadgets that we use every day, such as smart phones and tablet computers, needed programming. Even Cody's hearing aids were programmed with code!

Mr Chip then taught the Computer Club members some basic coding before they each practised on their computers.

Cody left Computer Club with his head buzzing! His first meeting had been brilliant. He realised there was much more to learn when he couldn't fix Brad's computer but he had no idea how much more!

Cody said goodbye to his new friends and hurried home. He was already looking forward to the next meeting.

Chapter 5: The competition

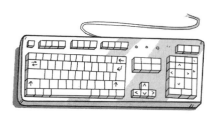

Week by week, everyone at Computer Club learned more about coding and Mr Chip gave them small projects to work on together.

Cody and Owen teamed up to make a light show, using a microchip and some tiny lights. They created a simple program that turned the lights on and off to the beat of Owen's favourite football chant.

Unfortunately, Owen loaded the wrong program from the computer and it made the lights turn on and off too quickly. One of the lights exploded and the microchip burst into flames.

Mr Chip leapt across the room to rescue what was left of the smouldering microchip. "How on earth did you do that?!" he laughed.

Owen shrugged his shoulders, looking a little embarrassed.

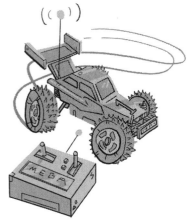

Cody also worked with Hana to make a basic remote-controlled car. She was very creative and thought of interesting ways to make it move, even adding a special button to make the car do an automatic U-turn.

They tested it in the classroom but the noise from the car's high speed scared the school hamster. "Oops. Sorry, Pickles!" apologised Cody.

After poor Pickles had calmed down, Mr Chip continued with the lesson.

He was so pleased with how the club

members were progressing that he had an idea.

"I want you all to show me how creative you are..." he told them. "If you create something that is really good, people might even pay you to use it!"

Everyone looked at each other. What was Mr Chip talking about?

"We're going to hold a Computer Club competition!" Mr Chip announced proudly.

Lucy was already keen to show off her skills and Hana started making notes of all her ideas.

"You are all to write a new computer program that will do something fantastic. I want each of you to create a prototype!" explained Mr Chip.

"What do you mean, *prototype*?" asked Owen cautiously.

Hana raised her hand to answer. "A prototype is like a sample. You make it to show others what your idea would be like if it was made properly."

The class fell silent. In all the excitement of thinking about writing their programs, they'd forgotten it was a competition. Surely, there would be a prize?

"The winner will receive my help to turn their prototype into a proper invention! For the rest of the school year, we will work together to make it something that can be used by everyone!" said Mr Chip.

Owen's eyes widened.

"Wowee!" he cried, pumping the air with his fist.

Lucy opened her mouth in disbelief – she was determined to win this prize! Meanwhile, Hana was still feverishly scribbling down ideas.

Cody thought about how awesome it would be to win - he'd never won a competition before. If his prototype was chosen as the best, everyone could play his game.

Cody was ready; he wanted to do everything he could to win. First, he had to do lots of research!

Chapter 6: Research time!

Later that week, Cody logged onto his laptop to look at websites where people buy video games. There were hundreds of different games!

Super Crazy Galaxy Invaders looked exciting but didn't seem to have a story. "This game might get quite boring after a while," imagined Cody.

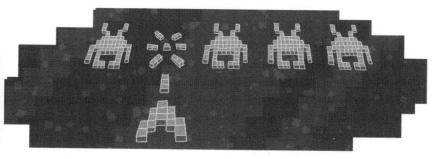

He thought *Secret of the Ninja Warriors* was far too violent for a kids' game (there was blood splattered all over the game's logo!).

High-Speed Wheels Deluxe was a car-racing game that looked like all of the other racing games. "I want my game to be different and stand out from other games," decided Cody.

Later that day at Computer Club, Cody furiously chewed the end of his pencil, struggling to think of the right questions to ask his friends at school.

"C-can I help you, Cody?" Hana whispered, nervously.

She had noticed his frustration. Cody shuffled across so that Hana could sit next to him.

"I think you should ask people what their favourite game is. Then you could ask about the things they look for when they buy games," she suggested.

He agreed and over the next few days, Cody asked all his friends and everyone at Computer Club about

their favourite games.

"Mate, my favourite would have to be *Mega-Football SuperKicks!*" shouted Owen. Cody shook his head and laughed.

"I don't like games much," said Lucy. "But I do play *Funky Donkey* on my phone. Everyone's playing it."

"There are lots of people who play games on their phone," Cody thought. "If people were able to download my game on to their phone, it would be really easy for them to buy it."

"I really like puzzle games," said Hana. "I enjoy games that encourage me to think hard."

This gave Cody an idea to create different challenges that got harder as the players made their way through the game.

Cody also asked his classmate, Brad. It turned out that Brad was a huge fan of games – lots of them, in fact.

"Dude, I love *Weapon Warfare Sixteen*. It's way better than *Weapon Warfare Fifteen*, but it'll never be as good as *Weapon Warfare Seven*. Oh, and

Sniper Shot is ace. Best game. Also, I play *Arch Wings* a lot. It's that space game."

Brad spoke really quickly but Cody noted everything down as best he could. Unfortunately, the battery in one of Cody's hearing aids began to run low and starting beeping loudly in his ear!

"What's your favourite style of game?" he asked quickly. BEEP!

"It's got to be shooting games, mate," replied Brad.
"Oh, and I love action games. You know, like *Bounty's Debt* or *Near Scream*."

BEEP! The battery was flat. Cody had managed to ask all of his questions in time but Brad was still talking.

All that Cody could hear was:"Mmph, mmph."

"Thanks for your help, Brad!" smiled Cody but he couldn't quite hear his friend's reply.

"Mmph!"

It had taken Cody a long time to collect all the research but he had an idea of what was popular and what type of game he should create:

He would make an adventure game!

He could explain to Mr Chip and the teachers that not many adventure games were available on the internet, even though lots of people liked them.

As Cody looked through his notes, he realised that all the games out there looked really cool and stylish.

Filled with doubt, he wondered how he would make his game look good. After all, he had no artistic skills whatsoever.

"Somehow, I need to get creative!"

Chapter 7: Get creative!

Cody set out to improve his creative skills but he knew it would take a lot of work. He was the first to admit that he was pretty awful at those lessons.

Cody was even dreadful at playing the triangle in

music. His hearing aids whistled whenever a high note was played and he always missed his cue. Sometimes, he pretended to play his triangle while everyone else in the orchestra played for real, but Mrs Quaver, the music teacher, could tell.

Cody was a terrible artist, too. In one art lesson, he tried really hard to draw an apple.

"It looks like some sort of animal or piece of furniture!" said a puzzled Mr Brush.

He wasn't much better at creative writing. Miss Fountain once asked everyone to write a poem about autumn. Cody's poem was, well, not good at all:

"Autumn is cold and rainy. Erm. The leaves are brown."

Miss Fountain did not enjoy his 'poem'. "Oh woe is me!" she cried

dramatically. "The spirit of autumn has been lost, Cody! I urge you to imagine the many golden colours of the leaves and the smell of bonfires in the air."

Cody rolled his eyes whenever she went over the top with her reactions.

But now Cody had good reason to work hard in creative lessons. It was time to focus.

In music lessons, he listened extra carefully to the sounds around him and when he played the triangle at exactly the right time Brad dropped his clarinet in astonishment. Mrs Quaver beamed – she was very pleased at his progress.

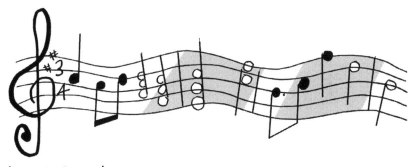

In art, Cody looked at the shape and shadow of the objects he painted. He chose his colours extra carefully, impressing even Mr Brush with his paintings.

When Miss Fountain asked the class to write a poem about winter, Cody wrote about gently falling snow and frozen lakes. He wrote about being home by a warm fire and drinking a steaming mug of hot chocolate.

"Oh, this is utterly marvellous, Cody!" Miss Fountain enthused.

After all his extra effort, Cody felt more confident and creative. His head was brimming with lots of cool ideas for what his game would look like and he was raring to start!

Chapter 8: Hunter Lion!

At the next Computer Club meeting, Cody looked at his notes. He'd done a lot of preparation and he'd even sketched his ideas for what the evil creatures would look like in his game.

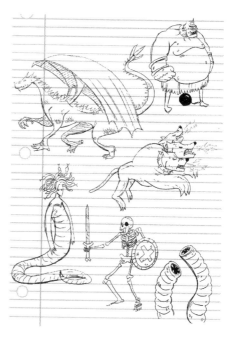

Now, it was time to turn those drawings into computer graphics.

He knew the coding had to be perfect. Mr Chip had told them that if anything was entered incorrectly, the game wouldn't work.

Cody decided to create the scenery first. He took his time as he wrote the code because he wanted it to look as amazing as the games in shops – even if it was just a prototype!

Sweat trickled down his face as he created a grand temple with secret doors, chambers and dungeons.

He didn't even blink for a while. The creation of Hunter Lion took ages but he managed to do it. Now he needed to test it!

It looked like the inside of a temple and there were pillars in the background and bizarre inscriptions on the walls but everything was dark blue. It needed to be sandy yellow!

"Uh oh," said Cody.

This was not a good time to panic. Cody breathed deeply and checked every entry in the code.

"Aha!" he cheered, when he eventually found the problem. He had written the wrong sequence of numbers. Phew!

Next he created the main character. Cody's research suggested that he should create a fierce creature rather than a human character. He decided to choose his favourite animal – a lion – and make it move like a human.

At least, that was what he hoped it would do. But when he pushed the button to make the character jump, it kept crouching on the ground.

"Why is it doing that?" he asked himself.

Once again, he checked everything but he couldn't figure out what was wrong. He needed help; Mr Chip came to the rescue.

He guided Cody through the code, making sure each piece was doing what it was supposed to.

"Ah, yes. You see there," he said, pointing to a group of words and numbers. "If you switch those words around, then your lion should jump properly."

Mr Chip was right - the lion hero sprang into action. It looked great!

Over the next few Computer Club meetings, Cody built his game using line after line of code. He

worked hard to fix problems and Mr Chip helped him out a couple of times. Cody made sure he never made the same mistake twice!

Finally, after hours of hard work and careful coding, he had finished making his own game. Now it was time to see if everything worked properly.

Nervously, Cody clicked the mouse to start the game.

The computer started to load the game.

He closed his eyes. He couldn't bear to watch.

Then he opened one eye.

He closed his eyes once again and waited a moment.

Then he opened both eyes.

It was working! *Hunter Lion* was ready to be played!

Cody was excited but doubt crept into his mind:

would it be good enough to win the competition?

Chapter 9: Competition time

Although everyone in Computer Club had spent a long time on their projects, Cody didn't know what anyone else had made, other than Owen, of course, who never stopped talking about his robot!

But now, it was time to reveal them. It was competition time!

All the teachers were invited to watch and vote for their favourite project.

They clapped and cheered as Mr Chip explained that he would help the winner to turn their idea into a product that could be used by other people.

Each club member really wanted to win. They glanced at each other but didn't say a word.

'Let's get started!" exclaimed Mr Chip. "First, we have Lucy."

Lucy stood at the front of the classroom to share her idea. She was very confident and looked like she was teaching the teachers. No lines were forgotten and everything was delivered loudly and clearly.

Lucy's prototype created strange images as music played. Mrs Quaver the music teacher and Mr Brush the art teacher applauded very loudly.

"You should choose *my* idea because it is the best!" exclaimed Lucy, without hesitation.

Cody started to feel a little anxious; he hoped he would sound as assured as Lucy.

Next, it was Owen. He had created a robotic leg that was designed to kick a football. He didn't say very much about his project and he hadn't planned a speech. Instead, he wanted to show off what he had made.

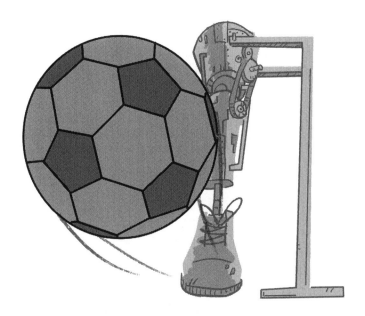

Everyone ducked as the ball flew towards them. Mr Aston, the sports teacher, cheered, and Cody gulped. Owen's demonstration was great!

Hana looked nervous when she stood up to do her presentation.

Hana stood next to a display of a chessboard and took a few deep breaths before beginning to speak. However, she was so quiet, people struggled to hear.

"Ch- chess is an old game and I wanted to m-make it really cool. I d-decided that when a player is about to capture the other player's piece, they have to answer a maths question," she stumbled.

The teachers leaned forward as they strained to hear what she was saying but there were lots of murmurs and nodding. They seemed to like the game, even if they couldn't quite hear Hana.

As soon as Hana realised they were interested, she became more confident and her voice became a little louder.

"A weaker piece such as a pawn could beat a queen in this battle if the player answers a more difficult maths question," she told the audience.

Cody sighed. "Hana is so smart. The teachers will love how educational her idea is."

Finally, it was Cody's turn. He gulped and walked to the front of the room. He was so nervous.

He could feel his heart thumping in his chest.

His hands grew sweaty.

His legs wobbled.

There were so many faces staring back at him, waiting for him to start. Would he mishear their questions and give silly answers?

He knew he had to calm down, so he closed his eyes, breathed slowly and opened his eyes again.

It was time to present *Hunter Lion*!

Chapter 10: Cody's game

Cody stood tall and began his presentation.

"Good evening everyone. I'd like to introduce a game that I have made. It's called *Hunter Lion*," he said confidently. "Could I please have a volunteer to play the game?"

He had practised his introduction well and was doing his best to hide his nerves.

Miss Green jumped up and down excitedly. "Pick me!" she shouted. Cody's heart sank. She panicked enough at computer errors, what would she do if an enemy character defeated her?

However, she was so enthusiastic that he gave in and agreed to let her play. Miss Green did a skip as she dashed to the front of the class to sit in front of the computer.

Hunter Lion's title screen appeared on the display. Some teachers started to murmur in interest and Cody could see that Mr Brush was interested by his design choices.

"As you can see, this game is set in an ancient world that is full of mystery and myths. I wanted to bring those ideas into my game so I created levels to be explored with secrets and dungeons." Cody did his best to sound loud and confident, just like Lucy.

Mr Brush smiled at the detail of the scenery, while Mrs Quaver quietly nodded her head along with the game's music. Miss Fountain liked the descriptions that popped up on the screen to tell the story, all perfectly

spelled and worded, of course.

Even Miss Green enjoyed herself until she faced a giant evil Cyclops on screen. She screamed as she tried to defeat the monster, ignoring everyone's giggles.

Cody explained how he had researched the games that were already available and asked people what they liked to  play. Mr Chip gave a thumbs-up to Cody for all the extra work he had done.

As Miss Green faced a difficult puzzle that involved symbols and letters, Cody took the opportunity to tell the teachers that the game was educational, too.

"There are many puzzles in the levels. These puzzles challenge the player and require them to think very carefully," he told them.

"I would like to thank Hana for suggesting this idea to me," he said looking over at Hana, who was hiding at the back of the room.

Mr Chip raised his hand to ask a question. "How would people buy this game?"

Cody remembered from his research that many people

downloaded games from the internet onto their games consoles or smartphones.

"I would sell it as an app for people to download," he replied confidently. "Without any need for boxes to store the game, it would be cheaper and easier to sell!"

Mr Chip wrote down some notes and nodded. He was impressed with Cody's response.

One of the teachers asked about his choices when designing the game and everyone nodded with approval at Cody's answers.

When Cody sat down, everyone applauded, cheered and waved their hands. (Waving hands is a way of clapping for people who can't hear very well.)

The clapping faded into silence as Mr Chip made his way to the front of the room. This was it. The presentations were over and now it was time for the vote.

Who was going to win?

Chapter 11: The results!

As the members of Computer Club waited nervously, Miss Green was heard shrieking and shouting. She hadn't stopped playing *Hunter Lion* yet! "I need to defeat the evil ancient vase!"

She rapidly pressed buttons on the controller and shouted at the screen. Some of the teachers had to wrestle her away from the computer.

"Come along now, Miss Green. We have to vote on the best project," laughed Mr Brush.

Although Cody could tell that Miss Green liked his game, he knew Hana's game was really good and was convinced that Mr Aston would vote for Owen.

No matter who won, Cody was happy that he had learned about coding. He had achieved so much already that winning would be a bonus.

Mr Chip collected little slips of paper from the teachers. Each slip was a vote.

Cody, Lucy, Hana and Owen stood at the front of the room, all smiling nervously.

Mr Chip hid in a corner of the room to count the votes.

The room grew quiet.

Mr Chip cleared his throat and walked slowly to the front. For a moment, Cody thought his hearing aids had stopped working because there was no sound in the room.

Mr Chip walked back and forth in front of the four club members.

"Aww, come on, Mr Chip," moaned Owen. "Tell us who won!"

Tension mounted as Mr Chip said nothing and continued to pace up and down. Then, he stopped in front of Cody. He reached out and shook Cody's hand.

"Well done, Cody. You won!" he smiled.

Cody's mouth dropped open in shock. He thought he hadn't heard Mr Chip properly but it was true. He had won!

"Everyone was very impressed with both your game and the way you presented it. I really think I can help you make it into an app for people to download. You did a fantastic job, Cody," said Mr Chip, proudly.

"I knew you were good with computers but you showed so many other skills. You did lots of research and worked hard in other subjects. In the end, you made a fantastic game that even Miss Green enjoyed."

"Well done, Cody!" cheered the teachers and the Computer Club members.

"Next, week we'll start work on making *Hunter Lion* into a real game for people to play!" promised Mr Chip.

*****

Cody had known a lot about computers before he met Mr Chip but as soon as he joined Computer Club, he began to learn so much more – and not just about coding and technology.

He had also faced his own fears and presented in front of a lot of people, not worrying if he would be able to hear their questions.

Now that Cody had won the competition, Mr Chip would help him to make his game into something that could be downloaded onto phones, or even sold in shops.

Cody was so happy. He wanted to carry on creating games because he loved it and was keen to make something for others to enjoy, too.

"I can't wait to get started!"

Code-it Cody is the second in the series of the Clever Tykes books. We really hoped you enjoyed reading it and be sure to check out the other titles in the series.

If you'd like to learn more about the Clever Tykes books visit www.CleverTykes.com. We'd love to hear from you!

You can even send an email to Cody and tell him what you think of his story: cody@clevertykes.com

You'll find us on Facebook (/CleverTykes) and follow Clever Tykes on Twitter @CleverTykes

Written by Jason, Ben and Jodie.

Made in the USA
Middletown, DE
14 September 2019